S0-BZH-731

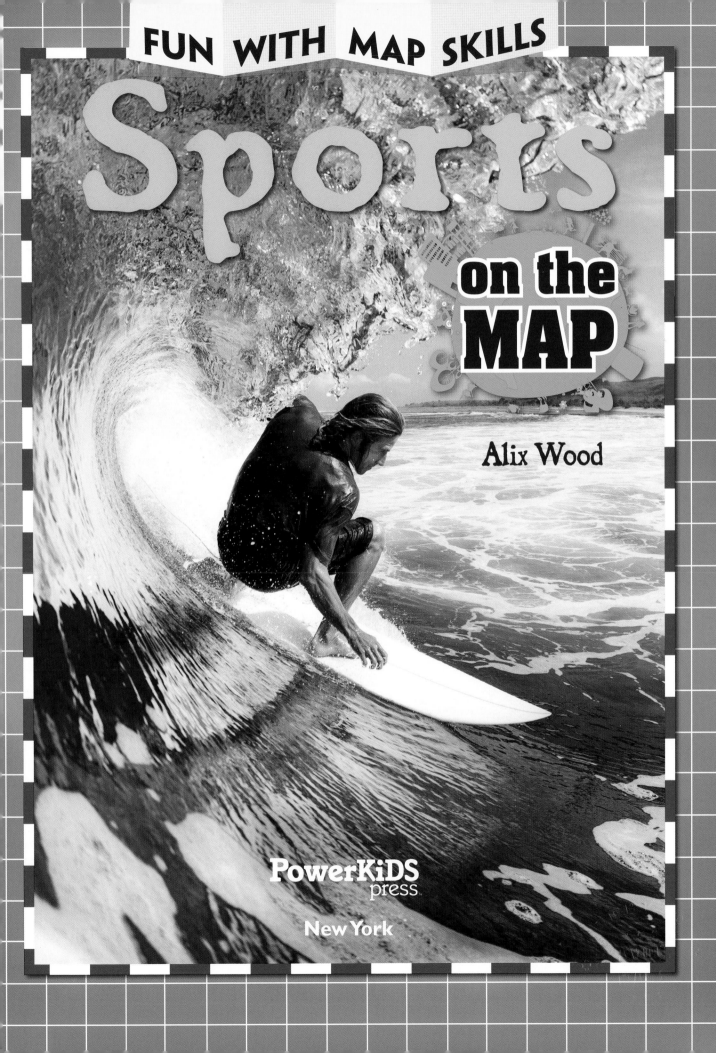

Sports

on the MAP

Alix Wood

PowerKiDS
press

New York

Published in 2015 by Rosen Publishing
29 East 21st Street, New York, NY 10010

Editor for Alix Wood Books: Eloise Macgregor
Designer: Alix Wood
US Editor: Joshua Shadowens
Researcher: Kevin Wood
Geography Consultant: Kerry Shepheard, B.Ed (Hons) Geography

Photo Credits: Cover © Herbert Kratky/Shutterstock; 18 Paolo Bona/Shutterstock;
26 © Rick Whitacre/Shutterstock; 29 bottom right g Mitch Gunn/Shutterstock;
7 top, 11, 21 top and middle © Alix Wood; all other images © Shutterstock.

Publisher's Cataloging Data

Wood, Alix.
Sports on the map / by Alix Wood.
p. cm. — (Fun with map skills)
Includes index.
ISBN 978-1-4777-6972-0 (library binding) — ISBN 978-1-4777-6973-7 (pbk.) —
ISBN 978-1-4777-6974-4 (6-pack)
1. Sports—Juvenile literature. 2. Navigation—History—Juvenile literature.
3. Maps —Juvenile literature. I. Wood, Alix. II. Title.
GV705.4 W69 2015
910.4—d23

Manufactured in the United States of America

CPSIA Compliance Information: Batch #WS14PK9: For Further Information contact Rosen Publishing, New York, New York at 1-800-237-9932

Contents

Do Athletes Need Maps?

There are many different kinds of maps and many reasons why athletes would need to use them. A map is a diagram of the Earth's surface, or of part of it. Maps record where things are in the world. It would be very difficult to travel to an away game without using a map. Some athletes need map reading skills to take part in their sport, too.

A globe is shaped like a ball, which is almost the same shape as the Earth itself. Because it is the same shape, a globe can show how the Earth really looks. It can't show you much detail, though. If you wanted to join your team in Europe from South America, a globe might be useful to see how far it was. Flat maps can be more useful than globes, however. They can fold up and go in your pocket or fit on your cellphone screen. Maps can show more detail than a globe because mapmakers can choose smaller areas to zoom in on.

▲ A globe can show an image of the whole world.

◀ A map can zoom in on a smaller area and show more detail.

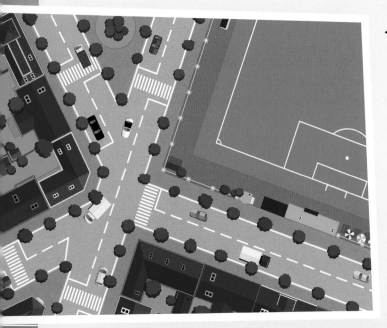

Do You Know?

The oldest known map is of the area around Babylon, in modern-day Iraq. It was made 2,600 years ago!

Maps are usually flat. People who make maps have to turn the curved Earth's surface into a flat drawing. These types of maps are called **projections**. They **distort** the shape of the continents a little. Mapmakers have to decide what view to have of the world and how to make a sphere into a flat picture.

▲ This projection shows a view from the North Pole.

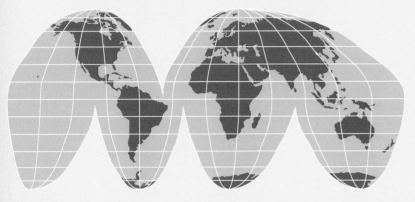

◄ This projection is called an orange peel projection. It looks as if the world was drawn on an orange and then the mapmakers peeled it off and flattened it out!

Which Map is Best?

Mapmakers need to decide what they want a map to show, and what can be left out. Imagine that you need to take part in these sports. Which map would be most useful?

1. You are taking part in a yacht race from Naples to Sicily.
2. You need to find the Heretown's soccer field.
3. Decide which area in Switzerland to go to for your skiing holiday.

b)
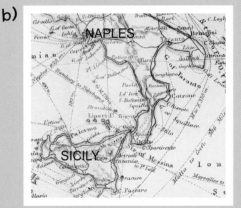

c)
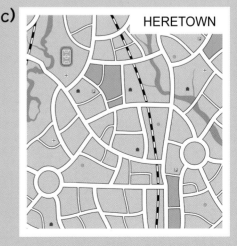

a)
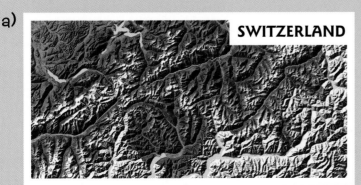

Keys and Symbols

The key on a map shows you what the **symbols** on a map stand for. Symbols are small pictures, letters, lines, or colored areas that show where things are on a map. Symbols need to be simple drawings that are clear when they are printed very small. A restaurant symbol might be a knife and fork, for example. A key is sometimes called a **legend**. Stadium maps will show spectators the way to things such as restrooms and food outlets. You are sitting in section B3. Look at the symbols on the right. Find where the nearest of each facility is on the map below.

Key	
	staircase
	restrooms
	disabled restrooms
	food and drinks
	first aid
	entrances
	escalators

Design Your Own Sports Park

All you need is some paper and pens. Design some simple symbols for each different sports arena you would like to see in your Sports Park. Draw a plan on some paper and place your buildings where you want them to go on the plan. Don't forget things like roads and trees. Put a key on the map so that people know what each arena is.

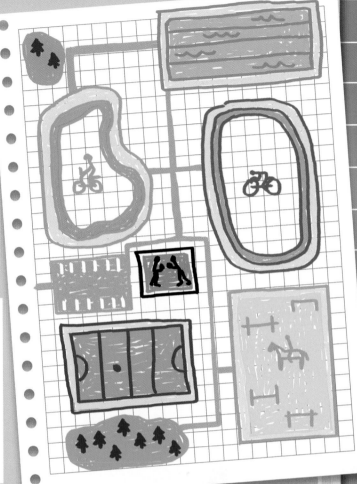

KEY

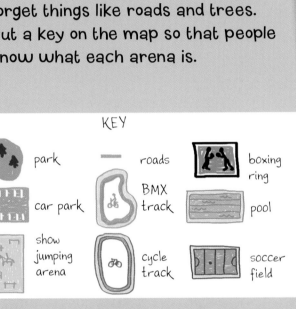

- park
- roads
- boxing ring
- car park
- BMX track
- pool
- show jumping arena
- cycle track
- soccer field

Try Your Skills

Symbols have to be simple drawings. Can you match the sports below to the symbols on the right?

1. ice skating
2. badminton
3. skateboarding
4. motor racing
5. baseball
6. weight lifting
7. judo
8. table tennis
9. boxing

a)
b)
c)
d)
e)
f)
g)
h)
i)

Gridiron Grids

Football is sometimes called gridiron because the lines on the field look like a grid. A grid divides an area into squares. Grids are used for map reading too. They make it easier to tell a person where somewhere is by giving them a **grid reference**. This reference number tells someone exactly what square on the map the place is. In football a grid can show the players and spectators how far along the field the players have run. Some sort of grid is used on most sports fields to mark out the playing area.

▲ A football field

To tell someone where something is on a grid, write down the number that goes along the grid first ⟶. Then write the number that goes up and down ↑. You can remember the order by saying "walk before you fly."

Do You Know?

You always write the number that belongs to the bottom left hand corner of the square.

y axis

Try Your Skills

To score a field goal you have to kick the ball between the two upright posts. Can you tell which of these grid references would score a field goal?
1. (5, 4)
2. (1, 5)
3. (3, 4)
4. (5, 1)

x axis

The football field on the right has been divided into a grid. The lines going across the page are the lines actually painted on the field. The lines going down have been added to make the grid complete. The numbers show how far it is in yards from the yellow 50 yard line to the end zone. A touchdown is scored when an offensive player takes the ball over the goal line into the end zone.

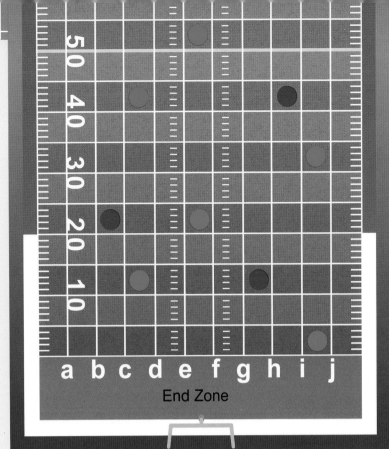

Your coach has written down some plays below. Each grid reference is a player. Each play involves three players. Can you tell if the blue team keeps the ball, or does the red team manage to intercept a pass? Which play ends closest to a touchdown?

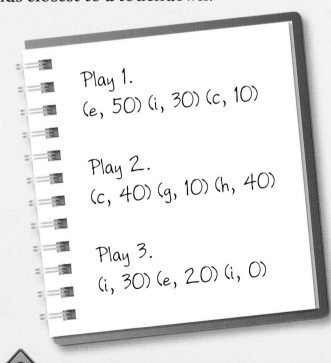

Play 1.
(e, 50) (i, 30) (c, 10)

Play 2.
(c, 40) (g, 10) (h, 40)

Play 3.
(i, 30) (e, 20) (i, 0)

Distance and Scale

A map's **scale** shows you how large the area is that the map covers. The scale lets you work out you how far one place is from another, too. Most maps will have the scale written on them. Maps are not the same size as the places that they show. The scale uses one unit of measurement, for example an inch to represent another unit of measurement, such as a mile. This scale shows 1 inch = 1 mile, 1.58 cm = 1 km.

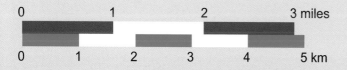

| 0 | 1 | 2 | 3 miles |
| 0 | 1 | 2 | 3 | 4 | 5 km |

A scale can be written as a **ratio**. The scale 1:10 means that one unit of measurement on a map is the same as 10 units of measurement in real life. A formula one race car is 15.2 feet (4.63 m) long in real life. This scaled-down picture below is drawn at a ratio of 1:25. That means that the picture is 25 times smaller than the car is in real life. Maps use scaled-down drawings to show large areas on a small piece of paper or screen. Everywhere on the map is the correct distance from everywhere else, just much smaller.

Do You Know?

Most maps will have a scale written on them. Look at a map and see if you can find the scale.

Try Your Skills

A large scale map shows a close-up view of an area in detail. A small scale map shows a large area in less detail. Do you need a large scale or a small scale map for the tasks below?

1. Your race team need to know how far it is from the Canadian Grand Prix to the Brazilian Grand Prix.

2. You need to find the pit lane at the Canadian racetrack.

1:25 scale drawing

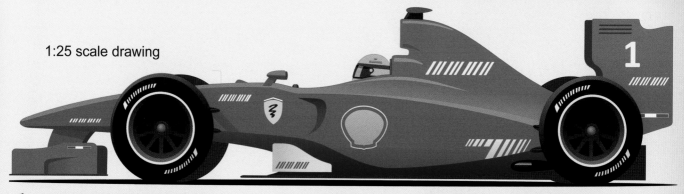

7.3 inches (18.52 cm)

Grand Prix Race

The racetrack on the right is staging a Grand Prix. The cars are going around the circuit. Can you answer these questions about the race?

Use the scale below to help you. Place a piece of string or cotton on the circuit to measure the distances between the cars. Mark the string at the middle of the first car's marker, and at the middle of the second car's marker. Then measure the marked string along the scale to find the distance between the cars.

1. What's the distance in miles between Team Red and Team Yellow?

2. How far ahead in kilometers is Team White from Team Blue?

3. How far in miles is Team Green from the finish line?

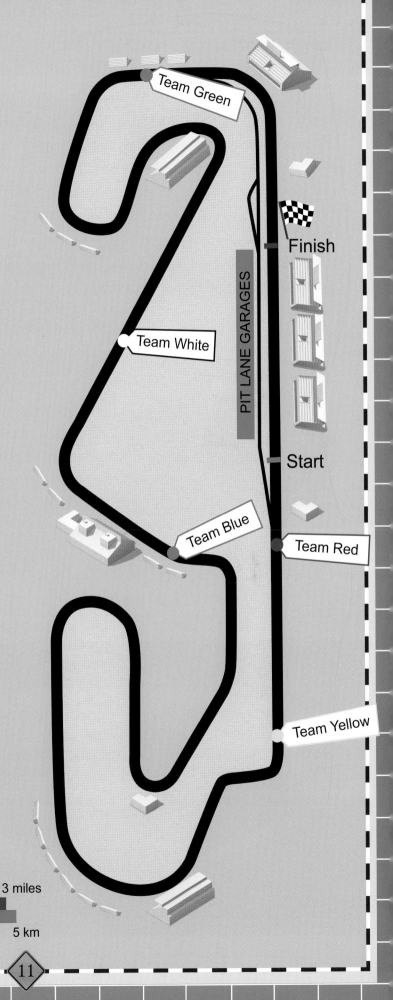

Team Green

Finish

PIT LANE GARAGES

Team White

Start

Team Blue

Team Red

Team Yellow

0	1	2	3 miles

0	1	2	3	4	5 km

Compass Directions

Compass directions help you get to where you want to go. The Earth is like a giant magnet. The north and south poles are magnetic. A compass has a magnetic needle which will always point to the **north magnetic pole**. Drawn on the compass is a **compass rose**. The compass rose shows the points of the compass. The four main **cardinal directions** are north, south, east, and west.

On most maps north will point toward the top of the map. If you go clockwise around the compass the main points are north, then east, then south, and finally west. They are usually written using just their first letter, N, E, S, and W.

Do You Know?

A good way to remember the points of the compass is that when north is pointing ahead, "west" and "east" make the word "we"

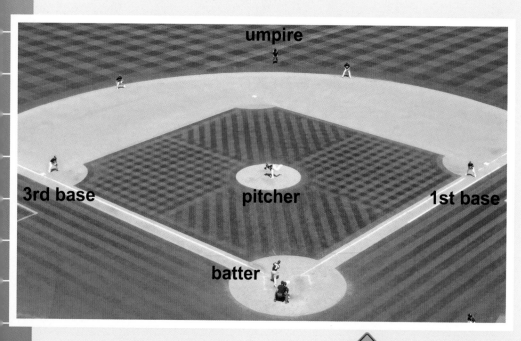

umpire

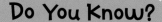

3rd base

pitcher

1st base

batter

Use the compass rose to work out in what direction this baseball pitcher's throws would go.

1. to the batter
2. to 3rd base
3. to 1st base
4. to the umpire

Intermediate directions are halfway between the four cardinal directions of north, south, east, and west. The intermediate directions are northeast, northwest, southeast, and southwest. They are usually shortened to NE, NW, SE, and SW.

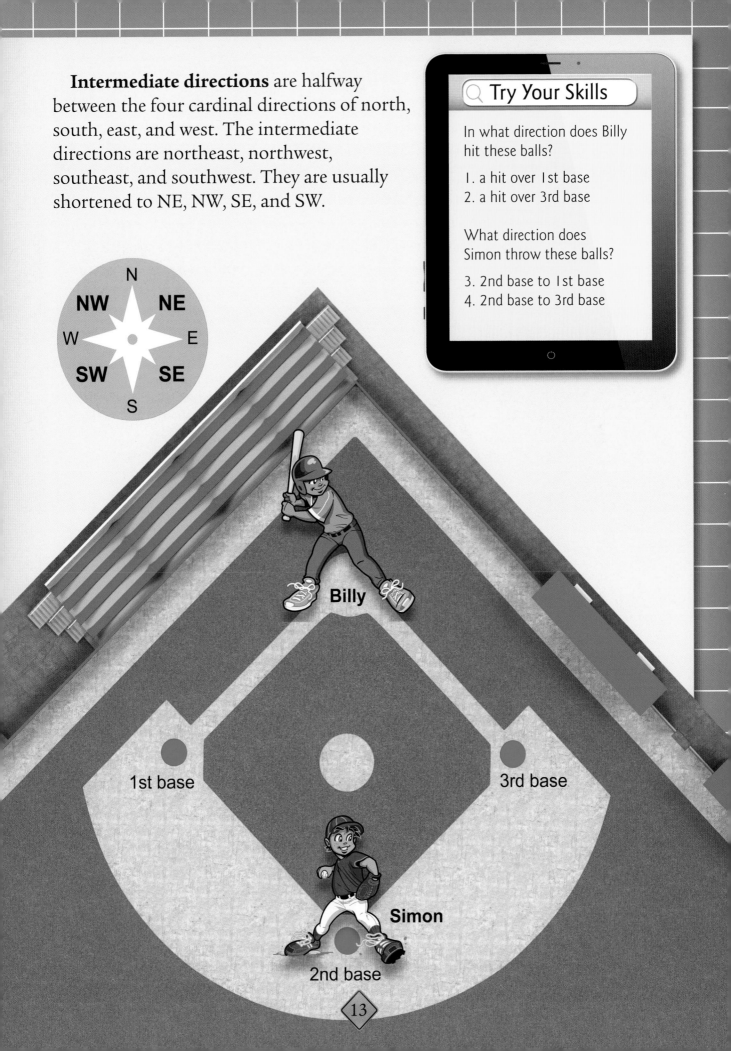

Try Your Skills

In what direction does Billy hit these balls?

1. a hit over 1st base
2. a hit over 3rd base

What direction does Simon throw these balls?

3. 2nd base to 1st base
4. 2nd base to 3rd base

Billy

1st base

3rd base

Simon

2nd base

13

Getting Your Bearings

A compass rose can also be divided into 360 **degrees**, just like a circle is in math. These degrees are called **bearings**. By using bearings you can be even more accurate than by simply using north or northwest. Imagine you are standing in the center of the compass rose below. You can give exact directions to somewhere else by giving the bearing to where you want to go in degrees. The bearings go clockwise around the compass rose. North is at zero degrees. East is at 90 degrees.

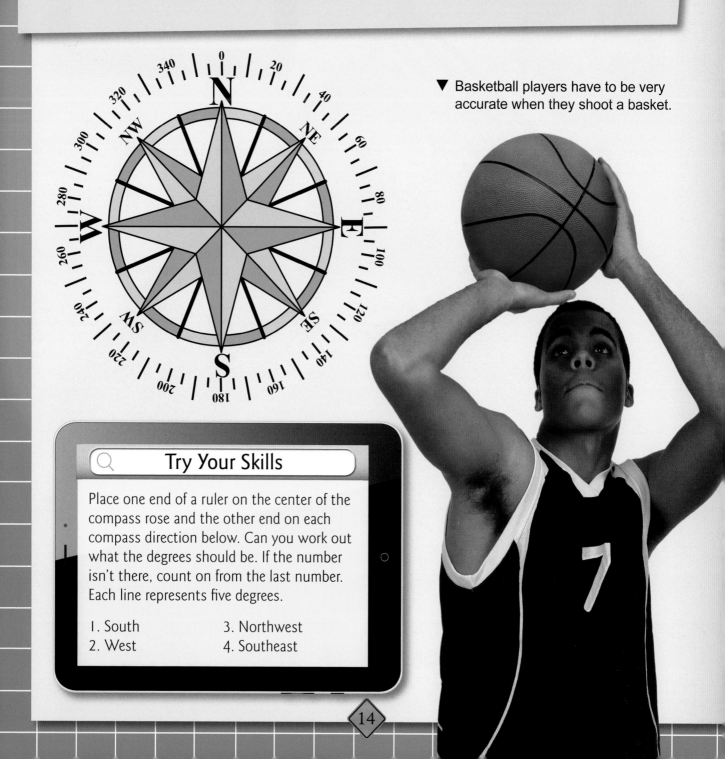

▼ Basketball players have to be very accurate when they shoot a basket.

Try Your Skills

Place one end of a ruler on the center of the compass rose and the other end on each compass direction below. Can you work out what the degrees should be. If the number isn't there, count on from the last number. Each line represents five degrees.

1. South
2. West
3. Northwest
4. Southeast

Shoot Some Hoops

Each colored circle in the compass roses above represents a basketball player. To make a pass, lay a ruler from the center of one of the player's colored circles to the center of another player's colored circle. Then read the bearing. Can you tell what bearings you need to hit the mark in these plays?

1. The blue player passes to the pink player
2. The pink player passes to the green player
3. The green player shoots a basket

Do You Know?

You can use degrees to find your way home on a walk. Try this. Walk 10 paces from "home" at a bearing of 30 degrees. Then walk 10 paces at a bearing of 150 degrees. Now walk 10 paces at 270 degrees and you should be back home.

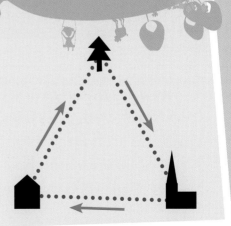

Slicing Up the Earth

Another way of finding places on a map is by using lines of **longitude** and **latitude**. Lines of longitude go from the top to the bottom of a globe. Lines of latitude go across the globe. Each line is numbered. Every place on a globe has its own special number which tells you where it is up and down the globe, and left and right on the globe. The north or south position on the lines of latitude is always written first.

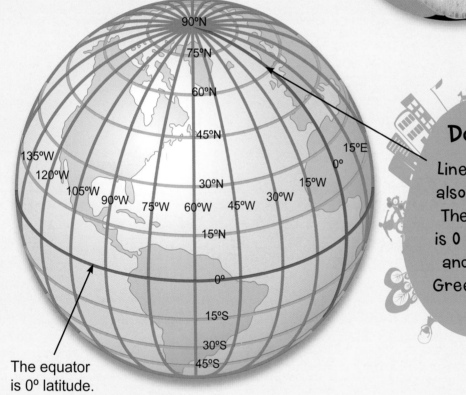

The equator is 0° latitude.

Any lines of longitude heading west from the prime meridian are written with a W after them. Any lines of longitude heading east have an E after them. The **equator** is 0 degrees latitude. Lines of latitude north or south of the equator have an N or an S after them. The word "degrees" can be written like this "°."

Where in the World is the Soccer World Cup?

Tom wants to visit some World Cup stadiums. Every four years the soccer World Cup takes place somewhere in the world. Plotted on the map below are the locations of some World Cups. But Tom has forgotten to put on whether the longitude lines are west or east of the prime meridian. Can you help him work out the longitude and put a W or E after the degrees? If a country crosses two longitudes, write them both down.

Where was :
1. the 1994 World Cup?
2. the 2002 World Cup?
3. the 2014 World Cup?
4. the 1966 World Cup?

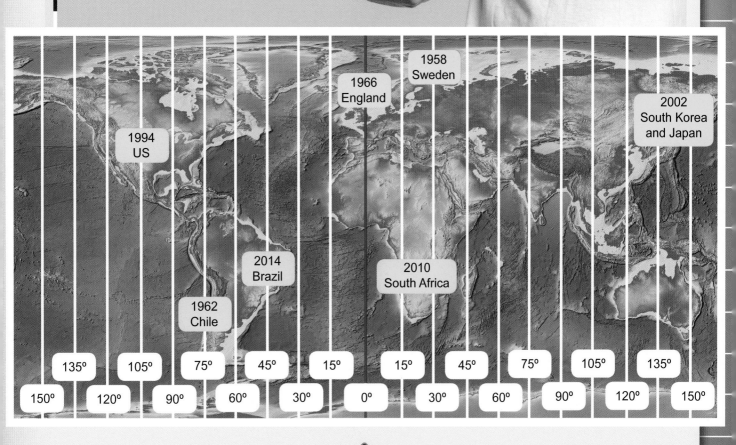

1958
Sweden

1966
England

2002
South Korea
and Japan

1994
US

2014
Brazil

2010
South Africa

1962
Chile

135° 105° 75° 45° 15° 15° 45° 75° 105° 135°

150° 120° 90° 60° 30° 0° 30° 60° 90° 120° 150°

North, South, East, or West?

The equator separates the Earth into two **hemispheres**. The northern hemisphere is above the equator and the southern hemisphere is below it. The prime meridian separates the Earth into the western and eastern hemispheres.

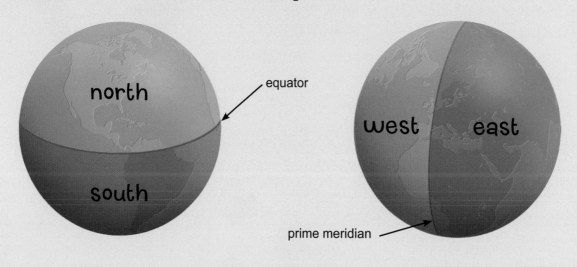

north

south

equator

west

east

prime meridian

In the sport of rugby, the northen hemisphere and the southern hemisphere teams are fiercely competitive. They play quite different styles of rugby. The weather in the northern hemisphere is usually colder and wetter. The southern hemisphere is dryer so the players are able to run more.

▼ A northern hemisphere rugby game can get a little muddy!

Do You Know?

Lines of latitude are sometimes called parallels. Parallel means things are always the same distance apart. Lines of latitude are parallel to the equator.

Try Your Skills

Look at the map below. Can you work out whether these rugby teams are from the northern or the southern hemisphere?

1. New Zealand
2. Italy
3. Argentina
4. US
5. South Africa

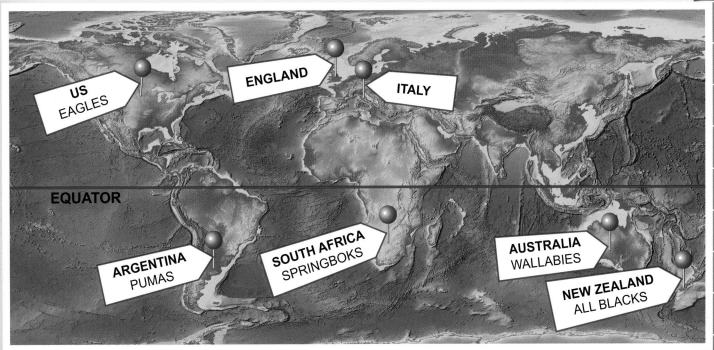

US EAGLES

ENGLAND

ITALY

EQUATOR

ARGENTINA PUMAS

SOUTH AFRICA SPRINGBOKS

AUSTRALIA WALLABIES

NEW ZEALAND ALL BLACKS

There are some other important lines of latitude. The Tropic of Cancer is 23.5° north of the equator, and the Tropic of Capricorn is 23.5° south of the equator. The Arctic Circle is at 66.5° north. The Antarctic Circle is at 66.5° south. The North Pole is at 90° north, and the South Pole is at 90° south.

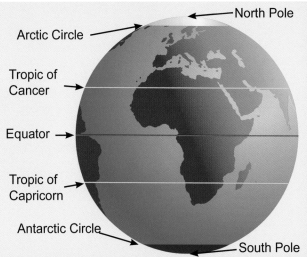

North Pole

Arctic Circle

Tropic of Cancer

Equator

Tropic of Capricorn

Antarctic Circle

South Pole

How High, How Deep?

Maps can show you how steep a mountainside is, or how deep an area of the ocean is too. **Relief** maps or **topographical** maps show these features. A relief map shows the hills and valleys by using shading. A topographic map shows the same information using contour lines. **Contour** lines link areas that are the same height.

Topographical maps can help you decide which slope to go snowboarding on. Snow Mountain is drawn below using contour lines. Each line shows what areas of the mountain are at the same height. When contour lines are close together, the slope is steep. When the lines are farther apart, the slope is shallow. Imagine that you could slice through a mountain at different heights. If you then traced around each slice centered on the same piece of enormous paper, that would make a contour map!

Try Your Skills

Look at the Snow Mountain contour map below.

1. Which slope is the gentlest slope to snowboard on, A or B?

2. Which slope is the fastest?

▲ Snow Mountain

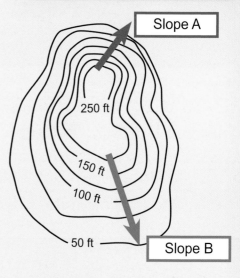

Slope A

250 ft

150 ft

100 ft

50 ft

Slope B

▲ Snow Mountain drawn using contour lines

Make Your Own Ski Resort

You will need a mixing bowl, 3 cups of flour, 1 cup of salt, 1 cup of water, 2 tablespoons of mouthwash, a large piece of cardboard, acrylic paint, and paintbrushes.

1. Mix the flour, salt, mouthwash, and water in a large mixing bowl. Add the water slowly until the clay feels like playdough. Add more flour if the mix is too sticky.

2. Place the cardboard on a flat work surface. Cover the cardboard with the clay and start to model your ski resort relief map. Make high areas for your slopes, and valleys for rivers to run through. Look at a map for inspiration.

3. Leave it for 24 hours to dry and then paint on the snow, rivers, roads, grass, and buildings.

Do You Know?

Relief maps can be made using satellite images taken from space. Images like this one show features such as mountain ranges and deep areas of sea. Do you think the sea is deepest when it is dark blue or light blue?